ISABELLA BREGA

Atlanta

APPOINTMENT WITH HISTORY

ATLANTA

CONTENTS

Text
Isabella Brega

Graphic design
Patrizia Balocco

Editorial coordination
Valeria Manferto De Fabianis
Alberto Bertolazzi

Translation
Ann Hylands Ghiringhelli

The Publisher would like
to thank the Georgia
Department of Industry,
Trade & Tourism, Barbara
Daniell, Liz Ratliff and
Diane Kirkland in
particular, for their
priceless help and
assistance.

This edition published in 1995
by Smithmark Publishers,
a division of U.S. Media Holdings,
Inc., 16 East 32nd Street, New
York, NY 10016.

SMITHMARK books are available for
bulk purchase, for sales promotion
and premium use. For details write or
call the manager of special sales,
SMITHMARK Publishers, 16 East
32nd Street, New York, NY 10016;
(212) 532-6600.

Produced by: White Star S.r.l.
Via Candido Sassone, 22/24
13100 Vercelli, Italy.

ISBN: 0-8317-0981-2

Printed in July 1995 by Grafedit,
Bergamo, Italy.

1 The gigantic Confederate
Memorial on the granite wall
of Stone Mountain is a
testimonial to Atlanta's glorious
past. The world's largest bas-
relief carving, it depicts three
Southern heroes of the Civil
War: President Jefferson Davis
and Generals Robert E. Lee and
Thomas J. "Stonewall" Jackson.

2-3 Atlanta, capital of the state
of Georgia in the Southern U.S.A.,
is a forward-looking metropolis
that has long shaken off the
ghosts of its confederate past.
Gone are the cotton plantations,
their place now taken by leading
multinational businesses.

4-5 For visitors to Georgia's
Stone Mountain Park, the huge
multi-attraction leisure venue
located about 25 kilometres east
of Atlanta, the atmosphere of the
"plantations era" is brought alive
by Antebellum buildings and a
paddlewheel riverboat. The most
prominent feature of the park is
Stone Mountain itself; the bas-relief
carving on the granite monolith
was completed only in 1972.

6-7 The huge Georgia Dome —
home to the Atlanta Falcons,
the local NFL American football
team — was completed in 1992
and is also used for conventions
and meetings.

8 Elegant homes in the old
suburb of Marietta, some
dating back to the mid-19th
century, are one of the many
faces of Atlanta, a city which
has always claimed to
epitomize American elegance
and good taste.

9 The bold, futuristic
buildings of Atlanta have been
in the vanguard of modern
architecture. Rebuilt around
the middle of the last century
after rising from its own ashes,
like the legendary phoenix,
the city is now ready for
future challenges.

10-11 The Capitol, built
in 1889 in imitation of the
Washington model. Atlanta
has always been the business
capital of America's Southern
States. The main target of
General Sherman's Yankee
troops during the Civil War,
in 1864 it was under seige for
117 days; its surrender was
followed by almost total
destruction. But in the space
of a few years it was on its feet
again, ready to resume its
leadership role.

(in documents of the Western & Atlantic Railroad Company). Perhaps for such a lively, industrious town a name with a feminine ring seemed more appropriate: whatever the reason, in 1847 its name was officially recorded as Atlanta. As the United States — and the railroad — gradually pushed westwards, Atlanta's importance as a railroad hub increased. And its ensuing growth also sealed its tragic fate. As the economic capital of the Old South, it became the pre-eminent target of General Sherman's Union army. In 1864 Atlanta was the scene of one of the fiercest battles of the Civil War. It fell after a siege lasting 117 days and Atlantans watched helpless as fires destroyed 90 percent of the city's 3,600 homes, together with all its shops, business premises and railroads. 5,000 of its 5,400 buildings were razed to the ground. But after only a few years Atlanta was on its feet and things were on the move again, as reflected in a famous saying attributed to the immediate post-war period: "Whether you're heading for paradise or hell, you have to change trains in Atlanta". Having arisen from the ashes like the mythical phoenix — which has since been its symbol — the city experienced periods of exceptional growth in the 1920-30s and 1960-70s, acquiring importance even at international level. It is now a forward-looking metropolis with a population of almost three million (including suburbs), about 63 percent African-American. It is home to prestigious educational institutions (including the highly reputed Georgia Institute of Technology, founded in 1880), manufacturers and multinationals which have together created one of America's leading financial and industrial cities and the foremost business centre of the Southern States. More than 430 of America's top companies, including Lockheed and Southern Bell, have offices here and among the businesses and organizations with headquarters in Atlanta are the American Cancer Society, Delta Air Lines, Coca-Cola, CNN and the National Center for Disease Control, the institution which identified and gave a name to AIDS. Atlanta boasts the biggest shopping mall in America's Southeast (Lenox Square has 200 stores and eating places), the biggest drive-in fastfood outlet, called the Varsity, and the

22 One of the galleries that are a characterizing feature of the Peachtree Center, the mastodontic shopping mall designed by local architect John Portman. In spite of its colossal size and its pervading impact on downtown Atlanta, the building is never oppressive or uninteresting.

23 top Boasting more than 22 kilometres of restaurants, stores, boutiques, cafés, fountains and suspended walkways, the Peachtree Center is directly linked with two hotels, the Marriott Marquis and Hyatt Regency, both also the work of Portman.

23 bottom The galleries of Atlanta's most celebrated shopping mall (its architecture has been copied the world over) give direct access to high-rise office buildings, garage facilities and even a rapid transport (MARTA) station.

24-25 The buildings created by Portman — an Atlanta architecture graduate of 1950 — offer spaces geared to the functional needs of pedestrians. The suspended walkways, for instance, allow people to get from one building to another without having to leave the cool of a climate-controlled environment.

world's biggest suburban car park, as well as the enormous Georgia World Congress Center, the world's second largest. A road, rail and air hub of major importance, it has an ultramodern, air-conditioned subway network carved out of the rock; in a ranking of airports worldwide, Hartsfield, Atlanta's international airport, comes sixth for air traffic and first for passenger terminal size (there is even an internal subway system for baggage collection). The downtown area with its tempting shopping plazas, fine hotels, restaurants and stores is dotted with futuristic skyscrapers and surrounded by ribbons of highways passing through residential suburbs and satellite-towns, some smart, others less so. The past of Georgia's capital is effectively represented by its Capitol, built in 1889 in imitation of Washington's better known model; its rounded gilt dome stands out among the longilinear buildings of downtown Atlanta. Situated in elegant Buckhead, the Atlanta History Center is one of America's foremost history museums. Also part of the Center is a vast site with other buildings of interest: Swan House, a lavish Anglo-Palladian Revival home built in 1928, with swan motifs concealed in the decorations and furnishings of each room; McElreath Hall, with its library and archives; and the simpler Tullie Smith House, a typical 1840 farmhouse which reveals something of the "sweat and toil" side of the Old South, the hard life lived by poor whites and so accurately described by Erskine Caldwell in the 1930s in "Tobacco Road" and "God's Small Acre". In the green of Oakland Cemetery, beneath the shade offered by marble statues of languishing maidens, lie soldiers who lost their lives during the Civil War. A reconstruction of the war can be seen in Grant Park: the Cyclorama is a massive cylindrical painting, 122 metres in circumference, dating back to 1885 and depicting the battle of Atlanta. A simple memorial stone instead marks the grave of Margaret Mitchell, buried here only a short way from the men she portrayed in her novel. A monument to the generals who led these same men is carved into the world's largest mass of granite at Stone Mountain, some 25 kilometres away, and it is one of the city's

26 In his attempt to give life to "pedestrian villages" in the heart of cities, Portman introduced a new design philosophy focused on developing buildings internally. Emblematic of this approach, the Peachtree Center has been a source of inspiration for other projects: Detroit's Renaissance Center, San Francisco's Embarcadero Center and Singapore's Marina Square.

27 Red granite alongside steel, marble and glass; cubes, cylinders and parallelepipeds; subtle touches or emphatic references to Art Deco or postmodern: the design features of many skyscrapers in downtown Atlanta give them a truly distinctive flavour.

main sights. In a vast leisure park covering over a thousand hectares with attractions including an original plantation of the 1800s, steam railroad, auto museum, five lakes, wildlife trails, restaurants and golf course, the enormous bas-relief, carved from the 251 metre-high monolith and measuring 58x27metres, commemorates the three Confederacy heroes: President Jefferson Davis and Generals Robert Lee and "Stonewall" Jackson. It recalls the gigantic sculptures of Mount Rushmore and is partly the work of the same sculptor: Gutzon Borglum. Old Atlanta also survives downtown in the fascinating Underground, a maze of streets and old buildings which escaped the ravages of Sherman's troups. Used as a hospital during the tragic battle of 1864, the area now offers a truly different shopping and entertainment experience. As well as the celebrated Zero Mile Post, erected on the site selected for the southern terminus of the Western & Atlantic Railroad and so official "birthplace" of the city, Underground offers a host of bars, restaurants, shops and night spots, amid a generally animated, fun-seeking atmosphere. There is a Bohemian flavour around Little Five Points too, with thronging crowds, noise and excitement. A different side of Atlanta is seen in the Fox Theatre, an extravaganza in Egyptian-Moorish style built in 1929 as a Masonic temple and subsequently converted into a movie house, with Arabian Nights décor. African-American Atlanta has close bonds with the Martin Luther King Jr Historic District. Five sites sum up the life and times of the civil rights leader and Nobel prize-winner assassinated in 1968: the unpretentious Victorian-style house where King was born in 1929, the Baptist church where he took over from his father as pastor, his simple white tomb set in a "Meditation Pool" and inscribed with the comforting words "Free at last", the nondenominational Peace Chapel and the Center for Nonviolent Social Change. Until the 1950s the Sweet Auburn district was the heart and soul of Atlanta's black community; home to the APEX Museum of African-American art, it was here that the WERD radio station and The Atlanta Daily World newspaper first got started.

28 The John Portman-designed Westin Peachtree Plaza, the world's tallest hotel (73 storeys): beneath its roof are gardens, cascading water, even a lake; in glass-encased tubes on its outer walls two elevators whisk diners to the Sun Dial revolving restaurant, practically at the very top of the building.

29 Rarely is an Atlanta skyscraper either anonymous or over-the-top. Reconciling technology and quality of life has always been a major concern here, and in 1982 the city was voted America's most human-scaled metropolis.

A T L A N T A

30 Streams of expressways and freeways crossing and orbiting the city are a reminder of Atlanta's strategic importance during the Civil War, when the railway made it the key Confederate ammunitions supply depot and consequently the primary military objective of the Unionists.

30-31 Downtown Atlanta's skyscrapers bear witness to its economic expansion. Capital of Georgia since 1868, barely four years after being razed to the ground by Sherman's troops, Atlanta underwent phases of accelerated growth around the years 1890-1900, 1920-30 and 1960-70, gradually increasing its importance internationally too.

Other city sites depict another face of black Atlanta: the Herndon Home, a 1910 mansion — with the ubiquitous white columns — built by Alonzo Herndon, the city's first African-American millionaire who founded the Atlanta Life Insurance Company; the residence of O.T. Hammonds, a renowned benefactor; Morris Brown College, one of Atlanta's oldest black institutions, whose most distinguished alumni include Maynard Jackson, Atlanta's first African-American mayor (1973), and film director Spike Lee. Business Atlanta is epitomized by the headquarters of Cable News Network, its newsrooms frenetically at work 24 hours a day, housed in the futuristic CNN Center, the realization of Ted Turner's biggest dream. The Center is packed with shops and eating places and a tour of the broadcasting studios ends at — no prizes for guessing! — the Turner megastore where visitors are greeted by gigantic reproductions of Hanna & Barbera's Flinstones. The World of Coca-Cola, with pillars contoured like Coke bottles, is the shrine of the world's best known soft drink, one of the most popular and now legendary products of 20th century consumer society. What lies behind net sales of almost $2 billion in 185 countries is related through historic documents, films, posters and the inevitable shop where you pay for the privilege of swelling the ranks of Coke testimonials. The millionaire Woodruff family — for over 60 years kings of the celebrated carbonated drink "invented" in Atlanta in 1886 by chemist John Stythe Pemberton — contributed generously to improving urban facilities, in particular Central City Park and the Woodruff Arts Center, currently home to several institutions, among them the Atlanta Symphony Orchestra and the modern High Museum of Art with its collection of American, European and African art exhibits. Atlanta's most recent hero, Jimmy Carter, also has a tourist-welcoming "monument". In the midst of a huge expanse of green, and offering a splendid view of the city, the Carter Presidential Center contains documents, photos and memorabilia of America's 39th president, plus a small-scale reproduction of the Oval Room in the White House. Not to be missed in this roundup of major Atlanta sites is the Michael C. Carlos

Museum of art and archaeology, the Sci Trek science and technology museum, the Observatory-Planetarium (with one of the world's largest telescopes) and the spectacular Ferbank Museum of Natural History. For younger visitors too (and the young-at-heart) Atlanta has plenty to offer: Botanical Gardens in Piedmont Park, Zoo Atlanta and Civil War fortifications in Grant Park, Center for Puppetry Arts, Toys Museum and — outside town — two theme amusement parks (Six Flags Over Georgia and American Adventures) and the nature reserve on the nearby Chattahoochee river. Having cast aside the provincial aspirations of the Old South that it once pursued in vain, thanks to the 1996 Olympic Games Atlanta's horizons are now thoroughly international. With the aid of 50,000 volunteers Atlanta threw itself wholeheartedly into the bid effort and now rejoices at this opportunity to say farewell to its stereotyped image of the past and to show the world what it is really capable of. Atlantans have not used the Olympiad as a pretext for radically re-designing their city; they have instead concentrated on constructing new sports facilities, like the Olympic Stadium, extending the airport and upgrading MARTA, the city transit system. Existing sports structures to be used for the Games include the Omni Coliseum arena, where the Atlanta Hawks basketball team plays, and the nearby Georgia Dome, which hosted the 1994 Superbowl and Peach Bowl and is home to the Atlanta Falcons NFL football team. The Atlanta Braves baseball team instead play at Fulton County Stadium, where new sports facilities are being built. In 1994 a fire destroyed "The Dump", as Margaret Mitchell herself jokingly called the unpretentious little house where the first part of "Gone with the Wind" was written. But Atlantans again have no intention of surrendering to the flames that appear to be part of their destiny and they hope the house will be rebuilt before long. The incident has in any case not affected their proverbial good humour. In a cartoon that appeared in The Atlanta Journal a few days after the fire, a small figure, pointing to the still smoking ruins of the writer's home, announced that as a tribute to Margaret Mitchell, her house had been officially designated as torch of the 1996 Olympic Games.

32-33 Underground Atlanta draws more crowds than any other city attraction. A downtown pedestrian precinct, it comprises six blocks built around the old railroad terminus. Today Underground is an amalgam of old buildings, shops, eating-places, street vendors and night spots, where a definitely bohemian atmosphere prevails. One of city landmarks within the confines of Underground Atlanta is the Zero Mile Post, starting point of the old lines of the Western & Atlantic Railroad, which the city was named after in the mid-1800s.

34-35 The World of Coca-Cola, a short way from Underground Atlanta, is a shrine to the world's most sold soft drink, "invented" in Atlanta back in 1886 by John Stythe Pemberton and first served, that same year, in Jacob's pharmacy.

36 One of the many events organized in Georgia's capital. An immensely popular sporting event (it attracts about 45,000 competitors) is the annual Peachtree Road Race, held on July 4.

37 left top From Picture Street, some of the most spectacular views of Atlanta's skyscrapers can be enjoyed.

37 left bottom Mitchell Street, named after novelist Margaret Mitchell, one of Atlanta's most dearly loved citizens — discovered by Harold Latham of the Macmillan Company — who wrote the amazingly successful "Gone with the Wind".

37 right The Flatiron Building in Mitchell Street, one of Atlanta's oldest skyscrapers. Ten storeys high, it was erected in 1897, almost five years earlier than the more celebrated examples in New York.

38-39 Mounted police patrol the city streets. The Atlanta of today is vibrant but not frenzied, restless but optimistic, futuristic but connotated by harmony and equilibrium, a city where industry and nature, modernity and tradition are each attributed their rightful place.

40 The Hard Rock Café, in centrally located Peachtree Street, is a favourite haunt of youngsters and tourists. Amid the rock iconography setting that is the chain's "trademark" are memorabilia of famous Georgia performers like James Brown and R.E.M.

41 left Atlanta Zoo, in Grant Park, is one of America's ten oldest, still operating zoos (it opened in 1889). Over 250 different species of animals from every corner of the globe can be seen there. As the name suggests, Ok-To-Touch Corral is very popular with the younger visitors. But baby gorilla Kudzu is the zoo's undisputed star.

41 right A lot of Atlanta eating and drinking places offer something really out-of-the-ordinary in the way of ambience: the Scrap Bar on Peachtree Street, for instance, is a kooky tribute to (or condemnation of ...) modern industrial society.

42-43 Atlanta Arts Festival, the city's most prominent cultural event, attracts over two million American and international visitors every year. It takes place in September in Piedmont Park, where the Dogwood Festival is held in spring.

42 Over a thousand performers, from traditional to avant-garde, appear in Piedmont Park in September during the Atlanta Arts Festival. Entertainment staged covers a broad spectrum of the performing arts including concerts and ballet. On the food scene, visitors can try gastronomic specialities from many different countries. The culminating event is the Artists Market, open every day from 11 am to 9.30 pm. The mood and events of the festival spread beyond the confines of the park, with exhibitions and "fringe" initiatives adding a lively note to fall in Georgia's capital.

43 top North of Underground is Central City Park, added to Atlanta's green facilities thanks to the generosity of Robert Woodruff, the Coca-Cola magnate who also financed the Arts Center that bears his name.

ATLANTA

44-45 Motor racing has a great following among the population of Atlanta. South of the city are Road Atlanta and the Atlanta Motor Speedway, considered two of the finest tracks in the country (and a bonanza source of income for the State of Georgia: close on $450 million a year). Around 30 automobile events take place at Road Atlanta annually while the Atlanta Motor Speedway hosts the Nascar Winston Cup, Hooters 500 (in November), Motorcraft 500 and the Nascar Busch Grand National.

46-47 The Atlanta Braves, the city's baseball team, train at Fulton County Stadium, situated south of downtown where new sports complexes host the Olympic Games. The Braves had a superb season in 1991, winning the championship, and did well in 1992 and 1993 too. The business triggered by this so-called "American team" is worth over $200 million a year to the city. The Atlanta Falcons, the local American football team, do their fair share too, with almost $90 million. Important roles in the life of Georgia's capital are also played by the Atlanta Hawks basketball team and the more recently formed Atlanta Knights ice hockey team.

48-49 Sacred and profane, religious fervour and big business, classical and modern: architectural opposites stand face to face in downtown Atlanta. On Peachtree Street and Peachtree Center Avenue the Gothic Revival belltowers and spires of the Catholic church of the Sacred Heart, the Baptist church and the Methodist church confront the mammoth volumes of the National Bank Building.

ATLANTA

50-51 Gospel music is the best known manifestation of the religious heritage of the city's African-American community. More black than white, Atlanta represents the "other half" of the United States. African-Americans account for about 69 percent of its population of almost three million (metropolitan area included). Known worldwide for the slave system depicted in "Gone with the Wind", Atlanta is also birthplace of Martin Luther King Jr, founder of the Civil Rights movement, and home to prestigious academic institutions like Morehouse College and Morris Brown College, one of the city's oldest schools, whose alumni include Atlanta's first black mayor, Maynard Jackson.

52-53 At Spivey Hall the huge organ dominates the stage of Atlanta's most celebrated auditorium. Its concert season is one of the most important in all America.

52 top Ebenezer Baptist Church, where first "Daddy" King, then Martin Luther King Jr served as pastors. With the nearby Martin Luther King Memorial, the nondenominational Peace Chapel and the Center for Nonviolent Social Change, it is one of main sites of the Martin Luther King Jr Historic District.

53 top The unpretentious Victorian-style house on Auburn Avenue — in the Sweet Auburn district, about a mile from downtown Atlanta — where the recipient of the Nobel Prize for Peace was born in 1929. He was assassinated in Memphis in 1968.

53 bottom A view of the grandiose façade of Spivey Hall: in its first three seasons some of the world's most famous performers appeared here.

54 top A display case in the Jimmy Carter Museum, where visitors can see memorabilia, documents, films and photos of the former president — in office from 1977 to 1980 — as well as a small-scale reproduction of the White House Oval Room. Here visitors can listen to Carter's recorded voice, relating memorable incidents of his presidency.

54 bottom Besides the Jimmy Carter Museum proper, where exhibits reconstruct the life of Carter as both a man and politician, the complex comprises a library, a convention hall, a chapel and even a small Japanese garden.

54-55 The museum, situated in a panoramic position at the centre of Inman Park, recounts the life and times of the 39th president of the United States, a native of Georgia whose family fortune came from peanuts, one of America's most important and celebrated crops.

55 Portraits of a youthful Carter, whose attempts to mediate in recent international conflicts like the war in ex-Yugoslavia, have brought him back into the public eye and given Georgia new standing in the political arena.

56 The huge dome of the Capitol, faced with 23-carat gold leaf from Georgia's Dahlonega gold mine and topped by a Statue of Liberty, holding the traditional flame. The statue was given to the city in 1884 by the State of Ohio, as symbolic compensation for the destruction wreaked by Sherman.

57 In the gardens surrounding the Capital are statues of famous sons (and daughters) of the State of Georgia: Joseph Emerson and his wife, Elisabeth Brown, for instance. The bronze monument to another illustrious Atlantan, Henry Grady, is instead in the heart of downtown. Orator and publisher of the "Atlanta Constitution", Grady gave voice to the interests of "The New South" — his most memorable speech was to the New England Society in New York — and, until his death in 1889, was a hero of the Reconstruction period.

58 Exhibits on display in
the Georgia State Museum of
Science and Industry. Building
work on the new Capitol
started in 1884, after a
subscription was launched
from the pages of a local
newspaper. Somewhat
curiously, this symbol of
the population's reaction to
the destruction of their city
by Unionist troops was built
by Ohio contractors.

58-59 As well as the Georgia
House of Representatives
and Senate, the Capitol houses
the Hall of Flags, the Hall of
Fame honouring outstanding
Georgians and the Georgia
State Museum of Science
and Industry.

59 An interior view of the Capitol's dome. Atlanta takes great care to conserve its heritage but its exceptional spirit of initiative has often kept it ahead of the times. Back in 1855, for example, it was the first city to use gas street lamps.

60-61 The Governor's Mansion, official residence of Georgia's governor, built in 1967 in West Paces Ferry Road. Constructed in neo-classical style by architect A. Thomas Bradbury, it follows the design typical of homes in the Southern States. In front of it is a small, octagonal square, with a fountain in the centre.

60 A view of the elegant gardens, also classical in their layout, with fountains, statues and neat hedges, situated on the west side of the property once owned by Robert F. Maddox, a former mayor of Atlanta. Seven of the mansion's rooms are open to visitors. Among the items on show is an outstanding collection of first editions of Georgian writers.

61 top The Mansion's 19th century furnishings, in neo-classical style, are mostly of American origin and are one of the finest collections of the Federal period (1825-1835). Set in the marble floor of the entrance hall is a large bronze medallion engraved with the State's motto: "Wisdom, justice, moderation".

61 center The State Drawing Room. The couch and mahogany table were made in New York; the mirror above the fireplace is late 19th century. Surrounding the entire building is a colonnade formed of thirty white Doric pillars.

61 bottom The bed of the guest room was made in New York, around 1815; the large carpet, of English origin, is dated about 1805. The panel above the bed is French, probably mid-19th century.

62-63 The classy homes of Buckhead — like those of Habersham, West Paces Ferry, Blackland, Andrews and Druid Hills — are fine examples of the variety offered by Atlanta's urban architecture.

A T L A N T A

64-65 Not far from Stone
Mountain Park are smart
shopping malls and exclusive
private clubs, set in vast
expanses of greenery to
the east of Atlanta.

65 In the years immediately after the Civil War there was a well-known saying which said: "Whether you're heading for paradise or hell, you have to change trains in Atlanta". Still today the city is a major hub for road and rail traffic, as proves the eight-lane highway to Stone Mountain Park.

66 An interior view of the Hyatt Regency Hotel, with its futuristic glass elevators in the foreground. Built by architect John Portman in 1967, with rows of internal balconies overlooking the atrium, it was the first example of a new approach to hotel architecture.

67 top left The Hotel Nikko, on Peachtree Road in the heart of Buckhead, is the ultimate in elegance and luxury. Inaugurated in 1990, it has 440 rooms and a choice of restaurants: Mediterranean cuisine with a French emphasis, or authentic Japanese.

67 top right A huge circular ceiling light dominates an atrium of the Colony Square shopping mall, at the entrance to the prestigious Sheraton Inn hotel.

67 bottom Phipps Plaza, on Peachtree Road, is one of the smartest shopping malls in town, crowded with elegant boutiques (Cartier, Saks, Tiffany, Gucci, Louis Vuitton), antiques dealers, specialty shops, art galleries and no fewer than five restaurants.

68-69 The ultra-modern High Museum of Art, designed by architect Richard Meier as a permanent home for the art collection formerly housed in the Woodruff Arts Center, founded by the millionaire Coca-Cola magnate whose generosity helped change the face of the city.

70 right Inaugurated on Peachtree Street in 1983, the High Museum of Art is the largest in town. Its collections are eclectic: paintings and sculptures from America and Europe (in particular, works from the Renaissance period), African and decorative art, photography, not forgetting the Spectacles children's gallery.

70-71 With around 7,000 items on show, the High Museum of Art is one of the most important in the south-eastern United States.

70 center and bottom In their thoroughly green setting, the Fernbank Museum of Natural History and Science Center offer exhilarating (and educational) experiences for young and old alike. The museum's many attractions include a permanent dinosaur exhibition, "A Walk Through Time in Georgia", the IMAX Theater with its gigantic screen, as well as a nature trail which takes visitors across almost 28 hectares of pristine forest.

71 The Fernbank Science
Center, which devotes much
of its room to dinosaurs,
has one of the largest
planetariums in the USA
and one of the most powerful
telescopes in the world
(in 1969 it transmitted the first
picture of Armstrong walking
on the moon).

72 The Atlanta Botanical
Garden is located in the north-
west part of Piedmont Park.
Among the many varieties of
flora to be found in its grounds
(occupying an area of 16,000
sq.ft.) are rare tropical and
endangered species.
Nature trails cross the garden
in various directions.

73 A well-known feature
of the Botanical Garden in
Georgia's capital is the
Dorothy Chapman Fuqua
Conservatory, opened to
the public in 1989: a garden-
lover's paradise of succulents,
carnivorous plants, tropical
blooms, bulbs, palm trees,
bonsai and exotic orchids from
far-away places like
Madagascar and the
Seychelles. Part of the plants
grow in huge conservatories,
the rest in the open. Atlanta
is famous for its parks and
gardens, with their dazzling
spring-time masses of azaleas,
magnolias and camelias.
Even the most futuristic
shopping malls have
ornamental hanging gardens
and tree-rich cloisters.

A T L A N T A

74-75 The Cyclorama in Grant Park is a fanciful Hollywood-style reconstruction of the battle which preceded the fall of Atlanta. It is a massive cylindrical painting, 122 metres in circumference and 15 metres high, depicting each phase of the tragic battle of July 22, 1864. Enhanced by light and sound effects and by models of soldiers, made from red Georgian clay, the Cyclorama rotates before the eyes of visitors standing on a viewing platform. Dating back to 1885-86, it was painted by a group of twelve Polish, Austrian and German artists.

76 CNN Center, hub of Ted Turner's broadcasting empire. Housed in the same complex as the CNN studios are business offices and restaurants; nearby are the Omni Hotel, Omni Coliseum (the 17,000-seater arena where the Atlanta Hawks NBA basketball team play and other major sporting events are held), Georgia World Congress Center and Georgia Dome.

77 A view of the newsroom operated round the clock by the CNN television network, one of the many offshoots of Turner Broadcasting System. The whole complex, situated in downtown Atlanta at the junction of Techwood Drive and Marietta Drive, is now a top tourist attraction. The 45-minute studio tour starts from the top of one of the world's longest escalators and offers tourists a fascinating insight into the world of the TV newsroom, where they can watch editors and producers frenetically at work (and even try their skills as "weathermen-women" in front of a TV camera). The tour ends, inevitably, in a megastore crammed with sweatshirts, caps, dolls and other paraphernalia bearing the unmistakable logo of Atlanta-based CNN.

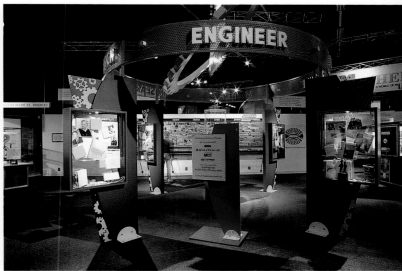

78-79 The Welcome South Visitors Center can supply every kind of information (about the Olympic Games and anything else) to tourists visiting Atlanta.

79 top Situated at the corner of Spring Street and International Boulevard, the Welcome Center is open — at different times — every day of the week.

79 center and bottom Cybermind Cobb, on Pleasant Hill Road, is a mind-boggling virtual reality experience. For kids in Atlanta there is also much of interest at the Science and Technology Museum (SciTrek), rated one of America's top ten science museums, where they can see — for instance — how phenomena related to the world of physics apply to ordinary everyday life.

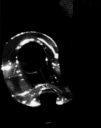

80 The World of Coca-Cola, a stone's throw from Underground Atlanta, is a unique "museum" with a collection of over 1,000 items advertising the world's most celebrated soft drink, the product-of-products of 20th century consumer society.

81 left bottom Flying over The World of Coca-Cola are flags of 185 countries where Coke concentrate is mixed with water, bottled and sold as the ultimate refreshing beverage, with net annual sales of some billion dollars.

81 left bottom And after visiting a "functioning model" bottling line, visitors to The World of Coca-Cola can head for the futuristic Soda Fountain where Coke flows "free", and then on to the well-stocked souvenir shop.

81 right bottom Besides the collection of Coca-Cola memorabilia, the museum tour includes a film highlighting aspects of what can be considered one of the biggest commercial success stories of the century.

81 right top Some of the many forms in which Coke has been — very effectively — advertised and promoted. To Asa G. Chandler, in the late 1800s, goes most of the credit for having turned Pemberton's magic formula into today's highly popular and profitable soft drink.

82-83 A general view of downtown Atlanta, with the CNN Center prominent in the foreground. Nearby is the enormous Georgia World Congress Center, the world's second largest capacity-wise.

"GONE WITH THE WIND" HISTORY VERSUS LEGEND

If you are in search of Scarlet, don't come to Atlanta. The elegant, sparkling capital of the Old South is now an ultra-modern metropolis which has long outgrown the image created first by Margaret Mitchell's bestselling novel and later by the even more successful film, interpreted by Vivien Leigh and Clark Gable. And yet this image has been little affected by the passing years and has now even been strengthened by the arrival of "Scarlet", Alexandra Ripley's sequel to "Gone with the Wind", promptly served up as a television serial. Both the serial and the book it is based on are lifeless shadows compared with the great and emotional tableau painted by Margaret Mitchell, who was profoundly attached to her native town and its people. It was purely for pleasure that she started writing the story in 1926, during a period of convalescence (she was then a reporter with the Atlanta Journal Sunday Magazine) and she initially turned down repeated offers from Harold Latham, New York publisher and talent scout. The historic events that centered on Atlanta left a permanent scar on its white heart: the horrors of the Civil War and the city's almost total destruction by Sherman and his Yankee troups, the hurt pride but unbowed spirit, the racial tensions of later years. And in spite of its skyscrapers and flourishing industry, Atlanta still tends to identify with the picture that was presented by Margaret Mitchell in 1936 and now forms the corpus of the Road to Tara Museum. The novel initially slammed by the critics and termed an "encyclopaedia of plantation folklore" proved immensely popular: 50,000 copies sold the very first day it was put on sale.
A book bought by 40 million people and translated into 35 different languages; a film seen by over 300 million, box-office record-breaker and winner of ten

84 The Road to Tara Museum is a shrine to the lasting legend of "Gone with the Wind", novel-turned-film, created in 1936 by the then unknown local writer, Margaret Mitchell. The museum also hosts photos of scenes from the film (its premier took place at Loew's Grand Theatre in Atlanta in 1939). In spite of its success (winning ten Oscars), Margaret Mitchell was never really happy with the film, especially the part about the rebuilding of Scarlett O'Hara's home, Tara.

85 Portrayed in a mural reproducing the poster of the film are its stars Vivien Leigh, who played Scarlett, and Clark Gable (Rhett Butler), together with Leslie Howard and Olivia De Havilland.

Oscars (though Margaret Mitchell was herself never happy with it, especially the part about the rebuilding of Tara). Admittedly the book can be described as tendentially racist, its black characters often stereotyped and denigratingly portrayed, its whites all misters and mistresses. But it tells the story of how — after the destruction of the Old South — the fighting spirit, enterprise and courage of the New South win the day. Atlanta resembles Scarlet — it was "... of her own generation, crude with the crudities of youth and as headstrong and impetuous as herself" — and it shares her determination to make a fresh start: "... they have burnt you down to the ground but they haven't destroyed you. They didn't manage to destroy you, and you'll grow big and beautiful, like you were before". Like the headstrong Scarlet, who has won a permanent place in its heart, the city stands its own ground, on both sides of the fence of convention, rebelling against conformity, a law unto itself, beautiful, confident and conspicuous, insolent but ingenuous, self-centred but generous, haughty but humble. Unable to accept defeat, spurred on by competition, the city prides itself on being the last remaining example of the lifestyle, elegance and good taste which helped create the fascinating legend of the Old South. It was a world in which everyone knew their place, on which the sun was eventually bound to set. But thanks to the Southerners' attachment to tradition, something has managed to survive. What prevailed in Scarlett's day were superficial formalities, first and foremost the gentlemanly, protective attitude of men towards women. For social etiquette had forced these women never to demonstrate greater intelligence than their menfolk and to contain their appetite in public because "young ladies who eat a lot don't find a husband". The very same women who, although stamped from early girlhood as "mere fragile, doe-eyed creatures"

86 The women of Atlanta occasionally like to identify with the fascinating protagonist of Margaret Mitchell's novel. Wearing the green and white dress made famous by Scarlett, Melly Meadows has travelled the world as an ambassadress of Georgia's capital, promoting its image far and wide.

87 A cruise across Stone Mountain Lake on a paddlewheel riverboat is one of the many pleasures — including walks, picnics, swimming, tennis, golf, fishing — offered to visitors to Georgia Stone Mountain Park.

89-89 Musical entertainment on board the boat from which — as an alternative to the steam train that travels a five-mile course around the mountain or ascent by cable-car to the top of the monolith — visitors can see more of the park's attractions.

90-91 An interior view of Wren's Nest, built in 1870 in Queen Anne style, home of Joel Chandler Harris, the writer whose tales about Uncle Remus were great favourites with American children in the latter part of the 19th century.

90 Wren's Nest, close to Atlanta, was the writer's home from 1881 until his death in 1908. A journalist on the staff of the "Atlanta Constitution", he chose this name for his house after finding a bird's nest in the mail box.

often found themselves, at only sixteen-seventeen years of age, with enormous properties to oversee, tens of slaves, clutches of children and hot-headed husbands. And Atlantan women today have lost none of the spunk of previous generations. They still treat the city streets as their oyster, but they like to furnish their homes along the elegant lines illustrated in Atlanta Houses and Lifestyles — comfortable couches with floral motifs, damask curtains, paintings and carpets, French or English furniture — and once in a while they indulge in a moment's bittersweet nostalgia, casting off their Chanel suits to don pretty bodices and crinolines. An indomitable spirit is still the distinctive trait of the city's female population. It is something the dynamic head of the city police force — with her ebony skin, jet-black hair and penetrating gaze — is clearly not lacking. Nor is the delightful Melly Meadows who, wearing a large straw hat and Scarlett's celebrated green and white dress and accompanied by her Rhett (real name Troy Baker, a police officer in Clayton), has spent two years touring the globe to promote the image of Atlanta. And spirit was certainly a quality shared by Margaret Mitchell, a small, bright-eyed lady whose fiction was based on thoroughly researched facts — obtained from diaries of Confederate doctors, documents and newspaper reports of the time — and on tales she heard told so many times as a child, by protagonists of those tragic events. And by voicing the viewpoint of the losers, she enabled them to recover their dignity, pride and consciousness of their role in history. When Margaret Mitchell was knocked down by a taxi and severely injured, almost 150,000 people knelt in the streets of Atlanta to pray for her recovery. She died on August 15, 1949 and — in the words of a local reporter — the sobs of Georgia were heard as far away as the Gulf of Mexico. The South was once again alone.

91 The building still has most of its original furnishings, including the table at which Harris sat to write his famous stories about Brer Rabbit, Brer Fox and other characters from the animal world. The stories of Uncle Remus are said to have been inspired by old tales that Harris heard related by slaves, when he was a child.

92-93 The mansion house of the Stately Oaks plantation, six-and-a-half kilometres north of Jonesboro, in Clayton county. Built in 1839 and now the headquarters of Historical Jonesboro, it is open to the public only on special occasions.

94-95 McNeel-Hamrick House, built in Greek Revival style in 1895, reflects a type of architecture much in vogue during the Civil War period. It is one of the finest-looking houses in Marietta, a town which started to develop north-east of Atlanta in 1834 and is now part of the city's urban sprawl. Marietta is deservedly renowned for its handsome buildings, part of them having survived the war and the destruction wreaked by Sherman. But already in the mid-1800s it was a popular resort, frequented by visitors attracted by its pleasant climate (tepid summers and mild winters) and the nearby spa where they went for cures.

SKYSCRAPERS

Built of red granite, glass, steel or marble, in the form of parallelepipeds, towers, cylinders or cubes and with echoes of neo-Gothic, Art Deco or postmodern, Atlanta's skyscrapers are definitely trendsetters. Located mainly in the downtown area, in the vicinity of the Peachtree Center — the tentacular shopping complex which captures the architectural spirit of Georgia's capital better than any other city building — these metropolitan giants overshadow but are not oppressive. The quality of metropolitan life has always been considered a major issue by city planners and architects, who made generous provision for green spaces and succeeded in reconciling the needs of technology and modern living. In 1982 Atlanta was in fact ranked as America's most

"human" city while in 1991 it was voted top business center of the whole USA. At the present time the capital of Georgia is considered fourth city worldwide for quality of life. The skyscrapers of Atlanta are imposing but never overwhelming, elegant but not excessively ostentatious, assertive but not threatening; practically all of them speak the same language, that of John Portman. Linearity, harmony and functionality are keynotes of the work of this brilliant architect whose passionate love of Venice can be seen in his attempts to reproduce the famous Bridge of Sighs in the suspended glazed walkways that link his buildings. His skyscrapers are not anonymous monoliths. Atlanta's irregular urban layout, based on the old railroad lines which criss-crossed the city, may have helped in this respect for the densely arrayed towers typical of so many American cities have been avoided and the distinctive characteristics of individual buildings are enhanced. The structures designed by Portman, an Atlanta architecture graduate of 1950, are much more than solemn statements which depend for impact on imposing volumes: they meet the need for urban environments offering the right sort of spaces for comfortable living. This talented architect has a great sense of rhythm and light and he uses them to create huge buildings but ones in which people can move

96-97 Atlanta's most original and celebrated skyscrapers are concentrated on Peachtree Street, one of the city's main arteries. Also on this street, north of the Peachtree Center, is Colony Square, an ultra-modern shopping mall: a series of structures made of marble, granite, glass and steel, but strictly in keeping with the "human-scaled" concept of architecture prevailing in Atlanta.

98 Vast expanses of glass, sparing use of concrete: the shopping malls most recently added to the metropolitan landscape — the Promenade II Building of Colony Square, for instance — respect the rules for human-scaled living spaces laid down by Portman in the 1960s.

99 top right Made instantly recognizable by its original gilt pinnacle, the skyscraper that houses the Atlanta offices of computer giant IBM overlooks Colony Square and is one of Atlanta's tallest buildings.

99 left Through the years the city's galloping economic growth has been reflected in its urban development: shopping malls, new streets and ever-taller skyscrapers have changed the face of Atlanta. And yet, as can be seen from this view of Colony Square, much of its original elegance remains.

about freely, naturally. Pedestrian man is the cornerstone of Portman's urban design philosophy. He built the Westin Peachtree Plaza, a towering cylindrical structure which is the world's tallest hotel and one of the most spectacular buildings in the USA: seventy-three floors with cascading water, lake, covered gardens and two external lifts, contained in "tubes" of glass, which in 80 seconds whisk guests to the Sun Dial, the revolving 70th floor restaurant from which, glancing downwards, you get the giddy feeling of having the whole city at your feet. Portman also built the Peachtree Center, Atlanta's ultimate symbol of architectural vision and business savvy. Like a giant octopus, this complex has gradually spread its tentacles over the entire centre of the city: among the structures "trapped" in its grasp are Peachtree Plaza, three of America's most stunning hotels, two office towers, assorted stores, a MARTA bus station, garage facilities and a dazzling, luminous shopping mall with over 22 kilometres of boutiques, restaurants, jewellers, cafes, fountains and splashes of greenery. This kaleidoscopic magic box offers visitors a seemingly endless succession of galleries, elevators, suspended glazed walkways, corridors and corners. And it expresses — more effectively than any other city site — the multi-faceted spirit of Atlanta, its determination to keep going, its delight in revealing its true nature little by little. With its superb combination of modern technology and polished style the Peachtree Center sets out to offer an exhilarating experience. It is not a claustrophobic container but a gigantic playground, a space where you can give full rein to your imagination, where you can live, eat, work and have fun without ever coming "down to earth". Two other awe-inspiring hotel buildings (besides the Westin Peachtree Plaza) form part of the complex. With its seemingly never-ending rows of undulating internal balconies, the Marriott Marquis (1985) resembles the huge belly of a whale; it has more rooms than any other hotel in the Southeast (1,674). The nearly-as-capacious Hyatt Regency (1967, over 1,300 rooms) is yet another outstanding example of modern architecture: balconies and windows overlooking an

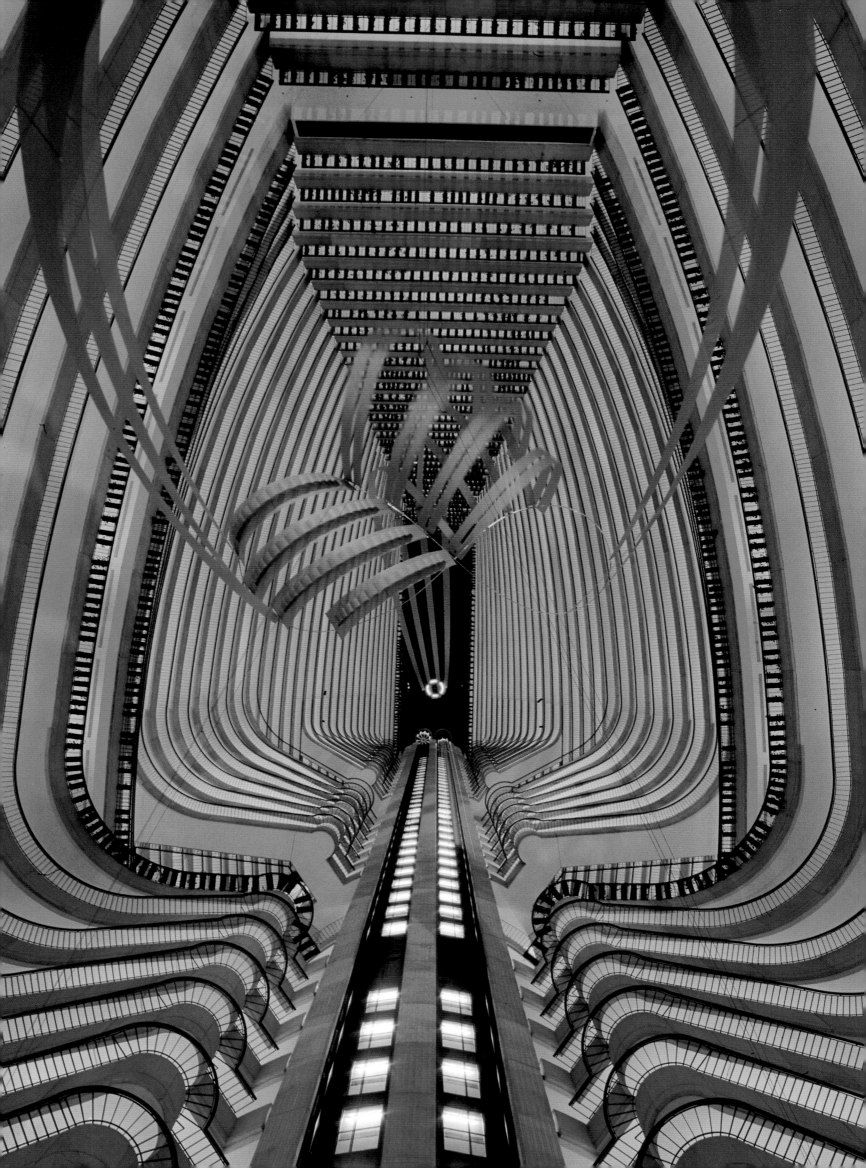

enormous atrium, external lifts encased in glass, Polaris revolving restaurant, sculptures, gardens and fountains. Two prototypes of a lifestyle fashioned by the humid heat of Georgian summers and reflected in architecture with an introverted focus: an approach copied in numerous other American hotels over the last two decades, some of them — like the Atlanta Hilton and Towers — located in this same city. Just as the architecture of recent years is luminous, light and airy, so the city's older buildings convey an aura of solemnity and equilibrium. The celebrated Flatiron Building, for instance, is a fine example of staggered volumes, with large windows, cornices and the ubiquitous white columns at its base. Constructed in 1897, five years before the first, more celebrated skyscrapers of New York, it has ten floors and was one of Atlanta's first high-rise buildings. The Macy Building, home of Macy's department store, dates back to the 1920s: both bulky and tall (though eleven floors of a recent construction would fit into its six), it denotes a thoroughly Americanized neo-Renaissance style; Italian workers were employed on building its façade. Even for this earlier generation of skyscrapers, the design focus of Atlanta's architects was on creating luminous, functional spaces: as long ago as 1927 the Macy Building, for instance, with its 189 metres of glazed cladding, had more windows than any other building in the world. Little has changed since then. Today the image of Atlanta is increasingly reflected in and magnified by its skyscrapers. Among the recent, noteworthy additions to the urban landscape are the IBM Tower — a tapered neo-Gothic mass 50 storeys high, topped by a gilt spire — and, in total contrast, the Georgia Pacific Building with its red granite stepped structure, seemingly formed of piled-up building blocks, liberally dotted with windows. With such a distinctive building for its headquarters, since 1982, the Georgia Pacific Corporation has not even felt the need to display its logo on the façade. By a quirk of fate it occupies the former site of Loew's Grand Theatre, where the world premier of "Gone with the Wind" took place in 1939. Once again the link between Atlanta's past and present remains unsevered.

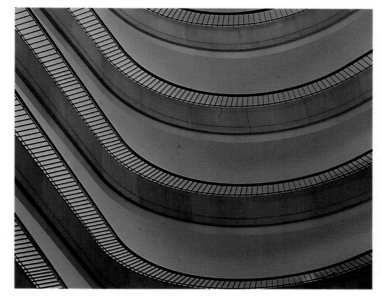

100-101 The atrium of the Mariott Marquis, a Portman-designed hotel adjoining the Peachtree Center and, for number of guest rooms, considered the biggest in the south-eastern U.S.A. Here, as in other projects by the progressive Atlantan architect, the elaborate interior spatial composition — with arrays of balconies overlooking the lobby — forms a major element of the overall design scheme, copied in many other American hotel buildings over the last twenty years.

102-103 The top section of the shining glass cylinder of the Westin Peachtree Plaza (inside is the celebrated Sun Dial revolving restaurant) contrasts with the gilt building here seen behind it.

104 The postmodern spire of the National Bank Building, one of Atlanta's numerous towering skyscrapers, its profile making a clearly defined contribution to the city skyline.

105 While trying to reconcile aesthetic impact, functionality, technology and quality of life, Atlanta's builders have always attributed great importance to illumination of interiors and energy saving. Among the city's tallest buildings are the Westin Peachtree Plaza, the Georgia Pacific Building and the One-ninety-one Peachtree Building twin towers.

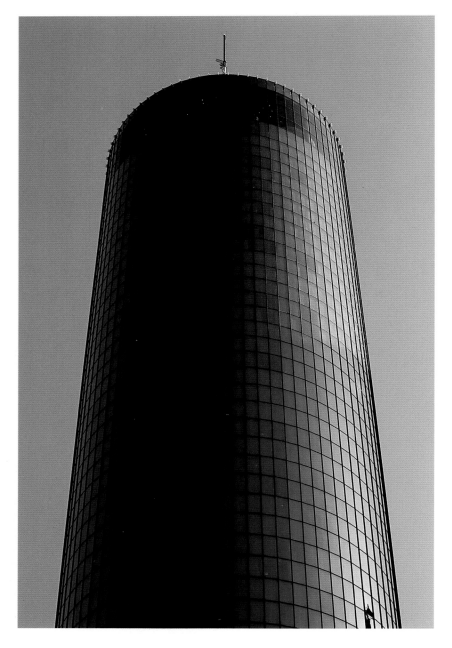

106 Thanks to its many futuristic hotels — like the Westin Peachtree Plaza with its 1,074 rooms — Atlanta is America's third-most-popular convention venue.

107 Two bronze sculptures of the Ballet Olympia add a graceful note to downtown Atlanta. They are adaptations of a work by Paul Manship, whose Prometheus stands in the Rockefeller Center in New York.

108 Projects by John Portman — in this case the shining cylinder that encloses the 73-storey Westin Peachtree Plaza — marked the start of a new approach to hotel architecture.

109 Inside the skyscrapers of Atlanta are the offices of more than 430 prominent American and multinational companies, making Georgia's capital one of the major business and financial centers of the United States and undisputed leader of the South. Among the many enterprises which have their headquarters in the city are Lockheed, Southern Bell, Coca-Cola Enterprises, Delta Air Lines, Georgia-Pacific, Holiday Inn Worldwide, Ritz-Carlton Hotel Company, Turner Broadcasting, the American Cancer Society and the National Center for Disease Control (the institution which identified and gave a name to AIDS, and sent teams to Zaire to fight the killer virus, Ebola). In 1991 Atlanta was designated America's top business city.

110-111 Tinged with pink at sunset is the National Bank Building, its graceful form set in a sea of Gothic Revival churches, colourful buildings in glass and concrete, and highways carrying fast-moving traffic: the cityscape offered by Atlanta may differ little from others of metropolitan America, but it is never boring.

112-113 Whether Gothic Revival, Art Deco revisited or postmodern, the metropolitan giants of Atlanta are never overstated or overwhelming. Part of the credit goes to the city's irregular street layout, which gives extra prominence to their individual features. Two more recent buildings have made a particular impact on the urban architectural scene: the IBM Tower, topped with a gilt spire, now one of the city's tallest skyscrapers, and the Georgia Pacific Building, an unusual composition of staggered red granite cubes, so easily recognized that its owners, Georgia Pacific Corporation, whose headquarters have been located here since 1982, have never even needed to display their logo.

114-115 Mirrored in the glazed circular tower of the Westin Peachtree Plaza are the rays of the setting sun and deformed reflections of the other high-rise buildings of the Peachtree Center, urbanistic heart of Atlanta.

AFTER DARK

Night works wonders for Atlanta. It tones down contrasts, attenuates the stress of a hard day, takes the edge off tensions between black and white communities which seem to have learnt to live side-by-side rather than together; it hides the squallor of rundown streets characterized by rusty automobiles, trash bins and rows of fire escapes; it enhances the beauty of old mansions and the elegance of upmarket residential districts.

The cool of the night banishes the oppressive heat of the day, bringing new verve to Atlanta as it dons its glamorous evening wear, content to put its frenetic

116-117 Darkness eases the tensions of a busy day as the city — its daytime inhabitants long gone to suburban neighbourhoods and nearby towns — dons its glamorous evening wear and parades all its finery.

lifestyle on hold while it contemplates its own finery and basks inmerited admiring glances. Once the roar from the freeways has died down and the hustle and bustle of the day has been forgotten, the city abandons its ultra-efficient façade and slows its pace to reveal another ingrained side of its nature. And like a tiring conjuror, it uses every trick of the trade to show off its wonders and charm its audience, in order to win an even bigger place in their hearts. Apparently abandoned by its daytime inhabitants, gone to sleeping suburbs, the great metropolis takes stock of its situation. And only then does nighttime Atlanta open her eyes — thousands of windows that had been blinded and closed to the daytime sun — and unhurriedly spread her carpet of light. Luminous signs — in ones, tens or hundreds — crowd the streets, and new noises and smells fill the air.

Rap, country & western, soul and jazz mix and mingle to produce the soundtrack of a city that never tires of its role as capital, ever alert to changing fads and fashions. Appetizing smells of fragrant fried Chinese titbits, Italian sauces, French mousses, Indian spices make our mouths water, while a kaleidoscope of

colours and lights makes us lift our gaze to admire astonishing arches of light, weird shapes, suspended illuminated galleries like entrances to mysterious spaceships. A shrine of nightime Atlanta is the Peachtree Center, its tentacles outstretched in an interplay of light and shadow, its soaring towers projecting beams of light down to the city streets and out towards the suburbs.

Life appears to be pulsating far above our heads as we stand on the ground, swathed in darkness, contemplating a fabulous world which seems to belong more to the gods than to men.

Night has spectacular effects on Atlanta.

After dark the city of skyscrapers prevails over the city of civil rights, of the affluent and the impoverished, of business and trade. Even at night the slim-line buildings of downtown Atlanta lose none of their individuality: they appear as gigantic cathedrals of light, irreplaceable landmarks in the black of night, pieces borrowed from a huge, magic puzzle.

Like precious embroidery shining through the velvety darkness, their crowning pyramids, spheres and pinnacles convey a new image, a different personality. They signal the victory of civilization, man's conquest of nature, symbolizing hope for the future.

Night brings a note of intrigue to Atlanta.

The stage left empty by the business hub of the Southeast is taken over by a world of senses and "vibrations". Gone are the earnest handshakes, replaced by furtively exchanged glances in the city of a thousand eyes: aggressive, insolent eyes of bands of youngsters; watchful, suspicious eyes of police patrolmen; glazed-over eyes of a drunk straddling the sidewalk; come-hither eyes of girls waiting in hotel lobbies. Tired eyes too, seen in a taxi's rearview mirror, restless eyes which stare for a moment from behind a car window, by the wavering light of a cigarette... Tomorrow is another day.

118 Georgia's futuristic capital is every bit the city envisioned by Henry Grady back in 1886. The famous publisher and orator put his case to U.S. public opinion in the following terms: "I want to tell General Sherman... that, out of the ashes he left us in 1864, we have created a fine-looking, courageous city; we have let the sun come shining into our homes but have kept out every trace of bitter memories or prejudice. The New South has devoted its every energy to the task in hand. A new breath of life animates its being. The vision of a better day illuminates its face".

119 Night descends over the colourful, futuristic World of Coca-Cola and over the nearby austere gilt dome of the Capitol, symbol of Georgia's past.

120-121 An evening performance in Chastain Park, one of the city venues best known for musical events. The summer concert series of the Atlanta Symphony Orchestra is held here.

ATLANTA

122-123 Built in 1929 as a Masonic temple and subsequently converted into a theatre, the Fox Theatre is listed in the National Register of Historic Places. Its bizarre architecture stems from a haphazard mélange of Egyptian-Moorish elements, with a dash of Art Deco. It seats 4500 and hosts concerts, musicals and motion pictures. A regular stop on guided tours organized by the Atlanta Preservation Center, its features include one of the world's largest theatre organs, with 3610 pipes.

124 A short way from the Georgia Dome, the Omni International arena is where the Atlanta Hawks basketball team plays; the arena also provides a venue for concerts and special events.

125 top Dante's Down the Hatch, on Peachtree Road, is one of the best-known and original eating places in town. The same adjectives can be used to describe its proprietor, Dante Stephenson. Pirate ship décor, with "all diners on deck". Excellent wine cellar, live jazz evenings.

125 bottom Every type of cuisine can be found in Atlanta. Here we see the exotic ambience of a Moroccan restaurant, its scenographic interior featuring carpets, low tables, scattered cushions and typically Oriental ornamentation. Dancers performing in traditional costume complete the Middle Eastern experience.

126-127 Having spread her carpet of light, Atlanta succumbs to the gentler, more relaxed pace of the city after dark. Ready to face another day.

128 Strange pillars with the contours of Coke bottles are a structural and decorative feature of the small pavilion in front of the museum which documents the century-long history of the famous beverage, first served in 1886 in Jacob's pharmacy in Atlanta.

ATLANTA

ILLUSTRATION CREDITS

All photographs by Antonio Attini except the following:
Georgia Dept. of Industry, Trade & Tourism: pagg. 1, 42 center,
42 bottom, 42-43, 44-45, 46-47, 50, 51, 117.